World War II in the Pacific

Susan Daddis & Michelle Jovin

Consultant

Jennifer M. Lopez, NBCT, M.S.Ed.
Teacher Specialist—History/Social Studies
Office of Curriculum & Instruction
Norfolk Public Schools

Publishing Credits

Rachelle Cracchiolo, M.S.Ed., *Publisher*
Conni Medina, M.A.Ed., *Editor in Chief*
Emily R. Smith, M.A.Ed., *Content Director*
Véronique Bos, *Creative Director*
Robin Erickson, *Art Director*
Michelle Jovin, M.A., *Associate Editor*
Kevin Panter, *Senior Graphic Designer*

Image Credits: front cover (all), p.15 (top) U.S. Navy; pp.2–3, p.5 (top), p.9 (bottom), p.10 (left), p.11 (bottom), p.18 (right), p.22 (left), p.22 (bottom right), p.24 (bottom), p.25 (left) U.S. National Archives; p.4 (bottom) William Vandivert/ The LIFE Picture Collection/Getty Images; pp.4–5 Roger Viollet/Getty Images; p.6 (top left) Library of Congress [LC-USZ62-40522]; p.6 Universal History Archive/UIG via Getty Images; p.8 (top) LOC [LC-USZ62-129812]; p.9 (top left/ right) National Park Service; p.10 (center) The Allied Graph, January 1944; p.11 (top), p.19 Keystone/Getty Images; p.12 LOC [LC-USZ62-128775]; p.13 (left) LOC [LC-DIG-ds-10891]; p.13 (right) U.S. Army; p.14 (right), p.15 (bottom right), p.17 (right) Naval History and Heritage Command; p.15 (bottom left) U.S. Air Force; p.17 (left) AP Photo; p.18 (left) George Bush Presidential Library; pp.20–21, p.21 (bottom) USMC Archives; p.21 (top) AP Photo/Joe Rosenthal; p.22 (top right) LOC [LC-USZ62-117122]; p.23 Los Alamos National Laboratory; p.24 (top), p.25 (top right) Everett Historical/Shutterstock; p.26 (left) Kyodo News via Getty Images; p.26 (right) Everett Collection Historical/Alamy; p.27 Lucas Vallecillos/Alamy; p.29 (top) Ryo Fukasawa/Flickr; p.29 (bottom) LOC [LC-USZ62-21027]; p.32 Jon Bilous/Shutterstock; all other images from iStock and/or Shutterstock.

TCM Teacher Created Materials
5301 Oceanus Drive
Huntington Beach, CA 92649-1030
www.tcmpub.com
ISBN 978-1-4258-5071-5

Table of Contents

World at War

It was the most destructive war ever. World War II involved more countries and cost more lives than any other conflict in history.

For the United States, World War II was fought on two **fronts**. In Europe, members of the military joined the Allied forces in the fight against the Axis powers. In the Pacific, the U.S. military fought a fierce air and sea war with Japan.

In the fall of 1939, German soldiers invaded Poland. That began the war in Europe. German troops took control of more and more land. Great Britain was one of the last European countries not under German control. The U.S. government sent weapons to British troops but stayed out of the fighting. Americans remembered World War I. They did not want to go to war again.

▼ Tens of thousands of buildings were destroyed in World War II.

Then, in 1941, Japanese planes bombed a U.S. naval base in Hawai'i. The attack left Americans with no choice—they joined the Allies in Europe and fought back against Japanese troops in the Pacific. That front ended with the first and only use of **atomic bombs** against a human population.

World War II changed the world. This is the story of the war's Pacific front.

Ready or Not

Before joining the war, the United States had been at peace for more than 20 years. It had only three **aircraft carriers** in the Pacific, and its pilots lacked combat training. The Japanese had been waging a brutal war in China. They had six aircraft carriers, and their pilots were highly trained.

Axis vs. Allies

World War II was fought between two groups. Japan, Germany, and Italy led the Axis powers. On the other side were the Allied forces. The Allies were led by Great Britain, the Soviet Union, and later, the United States.

Becoming Enemies

For Japan, the war did not start in Hawai'i. The small island nation had big plans, but it lacked resources such as oil, coal, and rubber. To get those supplies, Japanese soldiers invaded nearby countries.

In 1931, Japanese troops invaded part of China. Members from the League of Nations told the Japanese government to leave China. (The League of Nations was a group formed after World War I to settle disputes.) However, League members could not agree on stronger action. Japanese leaders quit the League and continued their invasions. Japan's troops killed hundreds of thousands of people in China.

Emperor Hirohito

The leader of Japan at this time was Hirohito (hee-roh-HEE-toh). He became emperor when he was 25 years old. He ruled for 63 years. Hirohito was the longest reigning emperor in Japan's history.

No Surrender

Japan's pilots and soldiers followed the *Bushidō* (BOO-shee-doh) code. *Bushidō* means "way of the warrior" in Japanese. One part of the code says fighters should value loyalty and honor more than their own lives. Japanese soldiers were expected to fight to the death.

Japanese soldiers celebrate their successful invasion of China in 1937. ▼

In 1940, Japanese troops invaded Southeast Asia. The U.S. government warned Japan's leaders to stop their attacks. President Franklin D. Roosevelt took further action. He placed a trade **embargo** on Japan. He also moved many of the U.S. Navy's ships to the Pearl Harbor naval base in Hawai'i. Hawai'i is between Japan and the mainland United States. The move was meant to be a show of force to Japan.

The United States stood in the way of Japanese leaders' dreams. So, they plotted to destroy the U.S. **fleet** at Pearl Harbor. Admiral Isoroku Yamamoto (ee-saw-ROH-koo yaw-maw-MOH-toh) came up with a plan.

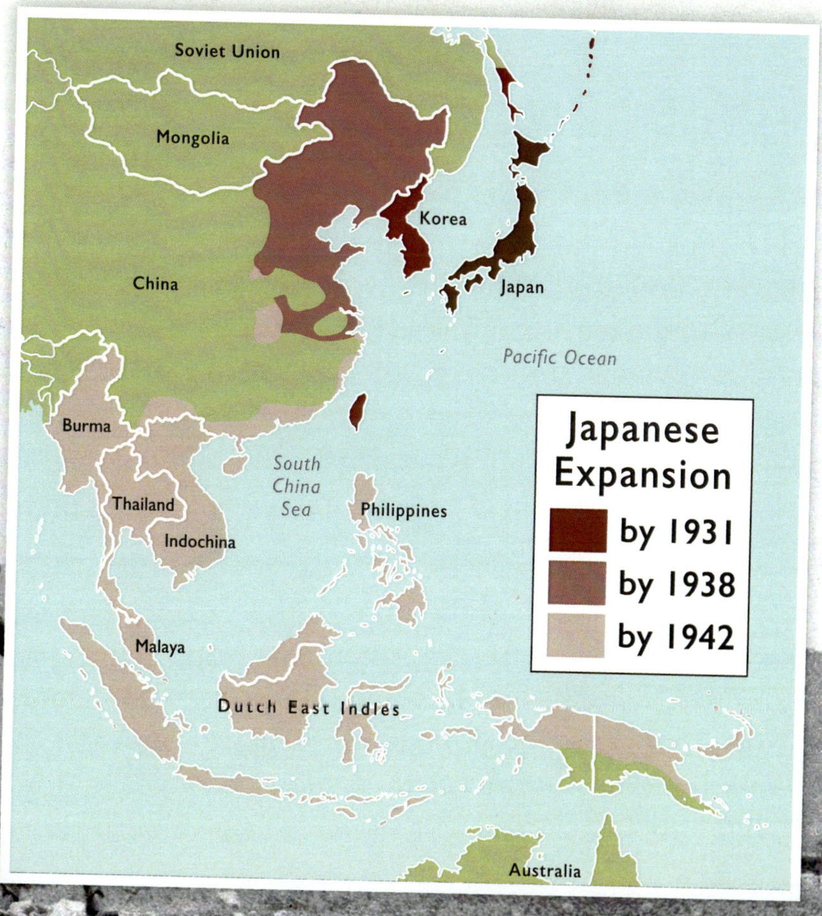

Surprise Strike

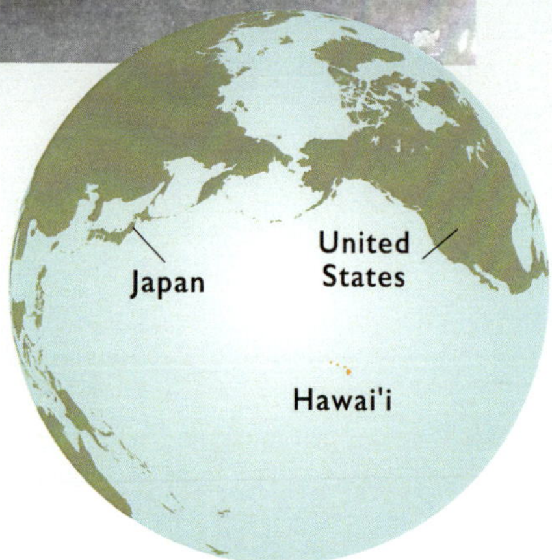

December 7, 1941, dawned quietly in Pearl Harbor. At the huge U.S. naval base in Hawai'i, almost a hundred ships sat anchored in the harbor. On local **airfields**, hundreds of planes stood in rows. Aboard ships, many sailors were sleeping late that Sunday. Others were eating breakfast. Suddenly, at 7:55 a.m., planes filled the sky. Surprised sailors saw red circles on the planes' wings. Japan was attacking!

Japanese pilots bombed the ships in the harbor. They also bombed nearby planes to stop Americans from fighting back. Black smoke filled the air. Burning oil covered the water as survivors tried to escape. One bomb struck gunpowder that was stored on the battleship *Arizona*. A massive explosion tore the huge ship in two.

▼ The USS *Arizona* burns after the attack on Pearl Harbor.

Brothers in Arms

Before Pearl Harbor, many U.S. sailors served on ships with their relatives. The explosion of the USS *Arizona* killed more than a thousand people. Among the dead were 23 pairs of brothers. After that, the U.S. Navy began recommending that family members not serve on the same ships.

The attack was over in two hours, but the losses were terrible. In all, 2,403 Americans died. Japanese bombs destroyed or badly damaged 21 ships. They wrecked about 160 planes. U.S. forces fought back as much as they could. But Japan lost only 29 of its 353 attacking planes.

▲ President Roosevelt signs a declaration of war against Japan.

The attack shocked Americans. Roosevelt said December 7 was "a date which will live in **infamy**." The next day, Congress declared war on Japan. In return, Japan's allies in Europe quickly declared war on the United States. The United States had fully joined World War II.

Fancy Pants

Two American pilots had been out dancing into the early morning hours of December 7, 1941. When the Japanese attacked, the men drove to a nearby airfield. They jumped in planes moments before they were bombed and took off. The pilots, still wearing tuxedo pants, shot down at least six bombers. They were each awarded a medal for their heroic actions.

Japan on the Attack

Within hours of the attack on Pearl Harbor, Japan's armed forces had struck again. Pilots bombed nations and islands in the Pacific Ocean. Most of these locations had large British and American military bases. Japanese leaders wanted to stop a counterattack before it began.

On December 8, bombers struck the Philippines. This group of islands was a U.S. **stronghold**. More than half of all U.S. planes in the Pacific were destroyed in the attack. Two days later, Japan struck again. This time, pilots bombed ships. U.S. leaders did not want to risk losing any more planes and ships. So, they ordered all large ships and planes to leave the Philippines. That left only a few fighter planes and small ships to defend the islands.

"I Shall Return"

General MacArthur was a brave soldier and a great military planner. He won a Medal of Honor for his defense of the Philippines. When Roosevelt ordered him to leave, MacArthur snuck out in a small boat. "I shall return," he promised the soldiers he left behind. Two years later, he did. Sadly, only a third of the soldiers he had left behind were still alive to see his return.

Code Talkers

To send secret messages in the Pacific, the U.S. Marine Corps recruited members of the Navajo Indian tribe. The Navajo language is very complex, and few people outside the tribe know it. The recruits came up with code words, such as using the Navajo word for *crow* to say, "patrol plane." Japan never cracked the clever code.

A Japanese soldier poses for a photograph at the invasion of the Philippines.

On December 10, Japanese soldiers invaded the Philippines on land. U.S. forces did not have enough soldiers to fight back. So, U.S. leaders began **withdrawing** their troops.

General Douglas MacArthur was in charge of the U.S. Army in the Philippines. Over the next few weeks, MacArthur brought his troops to safety on the Bataan Peninsula. He wanted to stay and fight. However, Roosevelt did not want to lose one of his best leaders. So, in March, Roosevelt ordered MacArthur to leave the Philippines.

General MacArthur

Allied soldiers on the Bataan Death March

March of Death

The remaining U.S. troops were trapped on the Bataan Peninsula. They had no easy access to food. They were forced to eat dogs and monkeys. Men were sick, but they did not have medicine. On April 9, the U.S. troops surrendered.

Japanese troops forced 76,000 Filipino and American soldiers to march to a prison camp. The march took place over the course of 66 miles (106 kilometers). The heat was brutal. Guards starved and beat the prisoners. Any man who fell behind was killed. Thousands of soldiers died during the Bataan Death March.

Behind Barbed Wire

In the United States, Japan's attacks scared people. Rumors spread that Japanese Americans were planning to help the enemy.

In early 1942, U.S. officials demanded that Japanese Americans living on the West Coast report to **internment camps**. Over the next three years, officials sent 125,000 people to camps in western states. Most of the people were U.S. citizens. Half were children. Officials imprisoned most of the internees until the war was over. When people finally left the camps, many had lost their homes and businesses.

▼ Japanese Americans are held behind barbed wire before being taken to internment camps.

Righting Wrongs

Internees felt the effects for many years. People pushed for the government to apologize. More than 40 years after the end of the war, Congress said the camps were a "grave injustice." Each survivor was paid $20,000 and given a formal apology.

Loyalty Under Fire

One army unit—the 442nd RCT—was made up entirely of Japanese Americans. Many of these soldiers had families in internment camps. Still, they wanted to join the war effort. The men fought bravely in Europe. The 442nd won more medals than any unit of its size in U.S. history.

▲ Sadao Munemori of the 442nd died in battle while his family was interned.

Turning Point

Early on in the war, Japan's soldiers won key battles in the Pacific. So, Japan's leaders turned to the Midway Islands. This was a U.S. base near Hawai'i.

First, Admiral Yamamoto would have Japanese troops attack the Aleutian Islands. Attacking this chain of islands would force U.S. ships at Midway and Pearl Harbor to respond. The Japanese Navy would then **ambush** the ships. Once the ships were destroyed, Japan would be free to attack Midway.

However, U.S. code breakers cracked Japan's secret code. They knew Yamamoto's plan ahead of time. So, naval leaders did not fall for the trap in the Aleutian Islands and instead sent three aircraft carriers to Midway.

Code Cracking

Just before the Battle of Midway, code breakers succeeded in cracking the Japanese secret code. To prove themselves, they sent out a false report. When Japanese leaders picked up and reported the false report, the code breakers knew they had it right. They persuaded the navy to risk its last three aircraft carriers in the Pacific. It was a big risk, but it paid off.

Finding Yamamoto

Yamamoto was Japan's top naval officer. In 1943, the United States **intercepted** a message about him. When code breakers decoded it, they learned that he would be flying to inspect some naval bases. U.S. forces attacked quickly. They shot down the plane, killing Yamamoto.

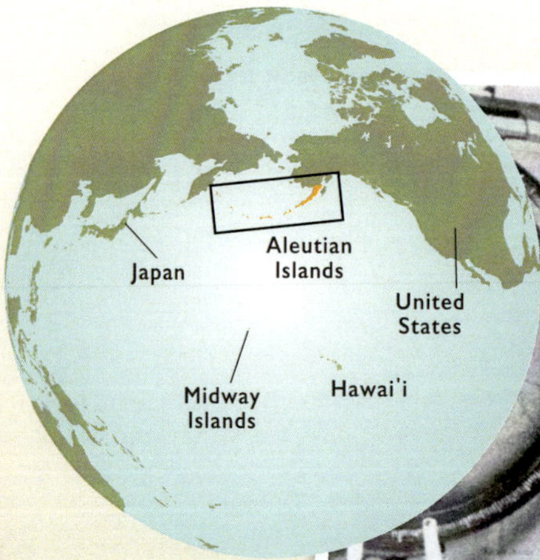

Admiral Yamamoto ▶

Pilots prepare to take off from an aircraft carrier before the Battle of Midway.

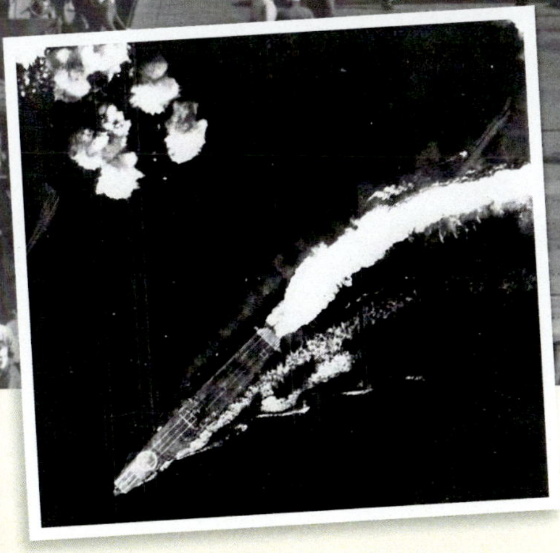

A Japanese aircraft carrier tries to avoid bombs at Midway.

Battle of Midway

On June 4, planes from Japanese aircraft carriers started to bomb Midway. Japan's pilots flew low over Midway. So, U.S. bombers attacked the planes from above. They quickly shot down most of the Japanese planes. U.S. bombers also struck Japan's aircraft carriers.

The Battle of Midway was a huge victory for the United States. Japan lost four large aircraft carriers and had 2,500 **casualties**. The Americans only lost one carrier and had about 300 casualties. This battle was the turning point of the war in the Pacific.

Fight for Guadalcanal

On July 6, 1942, Japanese troops invaded the Solomon Islands. From there, they could block sea routes between the United States and Australia. Japanese troops settled in. They began to build an airfield.

U.S. leaders were fresh off their victory at Midway. They wanted to take the Solomon Islands from the Japanese. So, on August 7, six thousand U.S. Marines landed on the islands. Private Al Dellaera was one of them. Years later, Dellaera remembered this day. "We got in a few hundred yards from the beach and then the Japanese opened fire on us," he said. "We were ambushed, really surprised."

Battles in the Solomon Islands raged on land and at sea. The United States was slowly taking islands one by one. Both sides had heavy losses, but Japan's were greater. Finally, after six months of fighting, Japanese troops withdrew from Guadalcanal. That was the last island in the Solomon Islands.

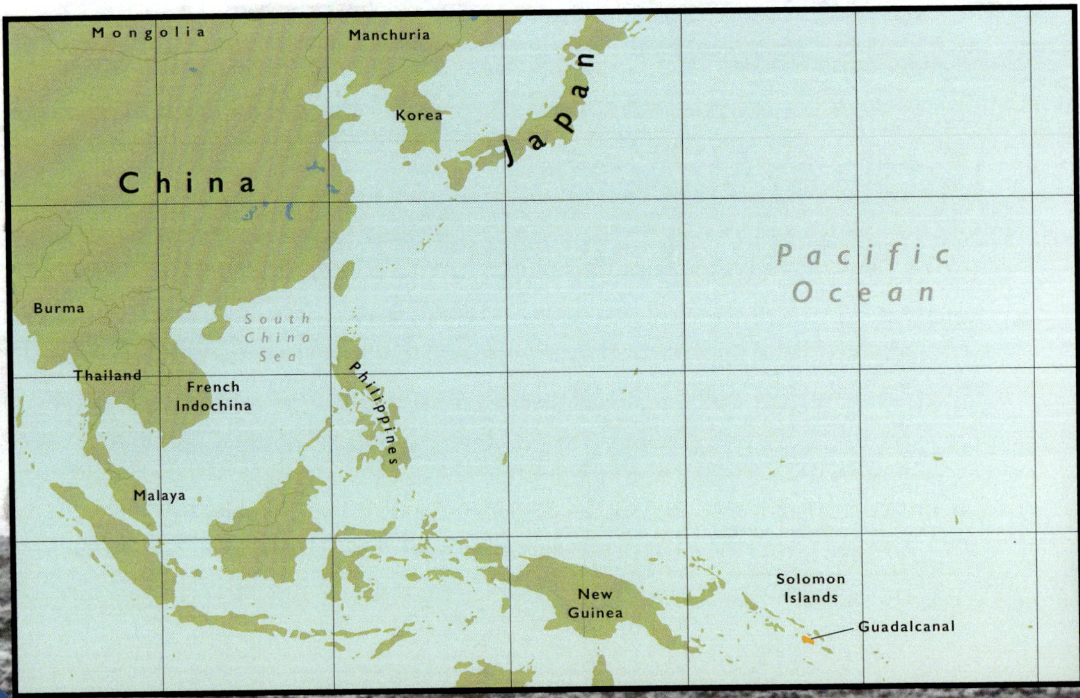

Island Hopping

The war in Europe was based on two huge invasions—in France and in Italy. However, the war in the Pacific was different. The United States and its allies landed on dozens of small islands held by Japan. This strategy was called *leapfrogging*.

Every island had its own risks, such as mountains, jungles, or caves. The Allies fought to take the islands one by one. Each victory moved U.S. forces closer to Japan.

▲ U.S. Marines charge the beaches on Guadalcanal.

Jungle Warfare

In the Pacific Theater, troops often had to fight in thick jungles. Many members of the armed forces became ill with **malaria** and other diseases. One common illness was a skin infection called *jungle rot*. Troops also had to deal with snakes and leeches.

Shipwrecked!

Before he was president, John F. Kennedy fought in the Pacific Theater. Kennedy was commander of a navy boat, the *PT 109*. After a Japanese warship rammed the boat, Kennedy and 10 other men swam to a small island. Kennedy carved a message for help into a coconut shell. Islanders took the message to U.S. soldiers, who rescued the men.

Retaking the Pacific

By 1944, most of the ships that had been damaged at Pearl Harbor were fixed. Naval leaders were ready to end the war. So, they sent ships across the Pacific.

U.S. Marines and soldiers forced Japanese troops out of different islands. Meanwhile, U.S. planes wiped out much of Japan's fleet of aircraft carriers. U.S. troops turned their attention to taking back the Philippines. They slowly moved closer and closer, taking Japanese-held islands as they went.

▼ U.S. Marines rest after taking control of an island in early 1944.

Suicide Bombers

As the course of the war changed, so did Japan's methods. In July 1944, Japanese pilots began using **kamikaze** attacks. Pilots would fly planes full of bombs into enemy ships. For the pilots, it was an honor to die for their country. Less than half of the bombers hit their targets, but the attacks killed thousands of Allied sailors.

Narrow Escape

Future president George H. W. Bush was a navy pilot in the Pacific. In 1944, he was bombing an island. Suddenly, his plane and several others were shot down. Japanese troops captured and killed eight U.S. airmen. Bush waited for hours in a rubber raft until a U.S. submarine rescued him.

▲ an injured Filipino woman and her baby during the Manila Massacre

The Manila Massacre

In February 1945, the Allies fought for control of Manila. It is the capital of the Philippines. The Allies had more soldiers than the Axis powers. The Allies thought it would be a quick victory. However, as the Allies won, Japanese troops became violent. They killed and tortured people who lived in the city. The Battle of Manila took one month. In that time, more than 100,000 Filipino citizens were murdered. This time is known as the Manila Massacre. Japan's leaders in Manila were later found guilty of **war crimes**.

Assault on Iwo Jima

U.S. leaders wanted to take the fight to Japan. However, they knew they would need an airbase to launch attacks. They chose the island of Iwo Jima for their base. It already had three airfields. And the island was fairly close to Japan's capital city of Tokyo. Japan's leaders knew they had to defend Iwo Jima at any cost.

U.S. planes had been bombing the island for months. In February 1945, 70,000 U.S. Marines landed on the island. Japanese troops had dug caves to defend themselves from the bombs. Progress was slow for the marines. Many of them died on the beaches.

U.S. Marines crawl forward on the beach of Iwo Jima.

The battle is famous for the fierce fighting on both sides. About 1 in 10 U.S. Marines died. Many more were injured. Japan paid an even higher price. Most Japanese soldiers fought to the death. Japan began with 21,000 soldiers on the island. Five weeks later, only 216 of Japan's soldiers were still alive.

In March, U.S. troops took control of Iwo Jima and started to bomb Tokyo. The bombs killed more than 80,000 people. In April, U.S. troops landed on Okinawa. After three months, that island was also in U.S. hands. The next target was Japan's mainland.

A marine runs as machine gun bullets hit around him at the invasion of Okinawa. ▼

Stars and Stripes

U.S. Marines landing on the beaches at Iwo Jima were met with intense gunfire, rockets, and bombings. They knew they had to make it to higher ground. On the third day, marines made it to the top of Iwo Jima's highest peak. There, they raised an American flag. Later, other marines returned with a larger flag. A photographer took a picture of the second flag being raised. His photo became one of the most famous images of the war in the Pacific.

Battle Days

Battles are often given letters to indicate the first day of the operation. The invasion of Okinawa began on "L-Day." The invasion of Normandy, France, one year before Okinawa is widely seen as the most famous "D-Day" operation.

Ultimate Weapon

On May 8, 1945, Germany's leaders surrendered to the Allies. The war in Europe was over. However, the war in the Pacific continued.

Three years earlier, President Roosevelt had approved plans to build atomic bombs. This work was known as the Manhattan Project. When Roosevelt died in April 1945, Vice President Harry S. Truman became president. Only then did Truman find out about the project.

Truman

The secretary of war requests a meeting to inform President Truman of the Manhattan Project. ▼

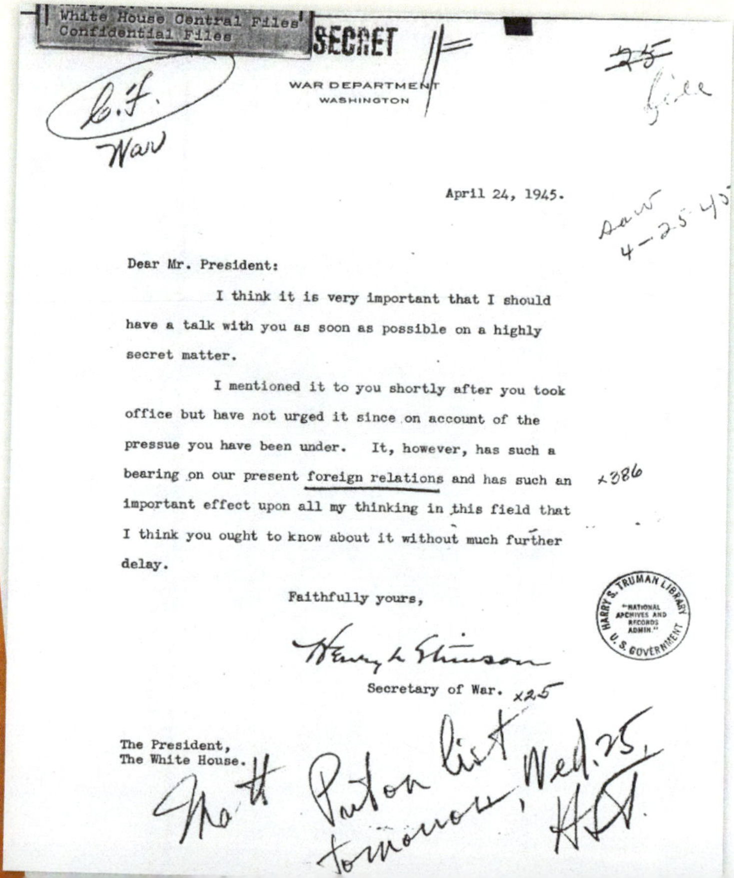

White House Central Files
Confidential Files

SECRET

WAR DEPARTMENT
WASHINGTON

April 24, 1945.

Dear Mr. President:

I think it is very important that I should have a talk with you as soon as possible on a highly secret matter.

I mentioned it to you shortly after you took office but have not urged it since on account of the pressue you have been under. It, however, has such a bearing on our present foreign relations and has such an important effect upon all my thinking in this field that I think you ought to know about it without much further delay.

Faithfully yours,

Henry L. Stimson

Secretary of War.

The President,
The White House.

Einstein's Letter

Albert Einstein wrote to President Roosevelt in 1939. Einstein warned that the Germans might try to make atomic bombs. When Roosevelt read the letter, he took the warning seriously. This letter led to the creation of the Manhattan Project.

"Destroyer of Worlds"

J. Robert Oppenheimer (above) was the lead scientist on the Manhattan Project. He later recalled the first atomic bomb test in the New Mexico desert. "A few people laughed, a few people cried, most people were silent," he said. A line from a Hindu text ran through his mind: "Now I am become Death, the destroyer of worlds."

Manhattan Project scientist near a test bomb in 1945

A Grim Choice

U.S. leaders wanted a quick end to the war. They thought many people in Japan would fight to the death to defend their country. An invasion of Japan was expected to cost up to half a million American lives. Many Japanese people would likely die in an invasion.

Truman knew atomic bombs would end the war. However, the impact would be **catastrophic**. Some people argued against using the bombs. They believed regular bombs and a naval **blockade** would force Japan to surrender. They said Japanese leaders were also looking for a way to end the war.

Truman decided to drop atomic bombs. Over the years, some people have called the bombings a war crime. Others believe it stopped an even greater loss of life.

"Little Boy" and "Fat Man"

On August 6, 1945, a U.S. plane—*Enola Gay*—rose into the air. It carried an atomic bomb known as "Little Boy." At 8:16 a.m., the plane dropped the bomb on the city of Hiroshima. A huge fireball wiped out much of the city. A **mushroom cloud** rose 7 miles (11 kilometers) high. At least 70,000 men, women, and children died instantly.

Three days later, a second U.S. plane dropped an atomic bomb called "Fat Man" on the city of Nagasaki. That blast killed over 35,000 people. Over the next few months, around 100,000 more people died as a result of the bombings. Many died of burns from the blasts. Other people had **radiation sickness**. On the same day of the Nagasaki bombing, Soviet leaders declared war on Japan.

model of "Little Boy" ▲

▼ The "Fat Man" atomic bomb is loaded onto a trailer for transport.

mushroom cloud over Nagasaki

Peace Monument

The Little Boy bomb destroyed most of the buildings in Hiroshima. Only one structure was left standing in the blast area. As people rebuilt, they kept the building as a memorial for all the people who had died in the bombings. It became the Hiroshima Peace Memorial Park.

Cranes of Hope

Many people who were exposed to radiation from the atomic bombs became sick and died years later. A girl named Sadako Sasaki survived the Hiroshima bombing but later became sick. She set out to fold 1,000 paper cranes. Doing that was supposed to make a wish come true. Sasaki's wish was to get better. Sadly, she died at the age of 12 from cancer.

Surrender

It was all over for Japan. Emperor Hirohito went on the radio on August 14. "The enemy has begun to employ a new and most cruel bomb," he said. Two weeks later, Japanese leaders signed surrender documents. As the news spread, people rejoiced. The war was over at last! The day of victory became known as V-J Day.

Post-War World

World War II came at a great cost. The Pacific Theater was brutal. Almost three million Japanese people died. Huge parts of the country were destroyed.

For seven years after the war, the Allies controlled Japan. For the first couple of years, the Allies' main goal was to break up the military. In 1947, the Allies' purpose began to change. Allied leaders worked to rebuild Japan's economy. They also wanted Japan to be a democracy. General MacArthur was put in charge of helping Japan form a democracy. With his help, Japanese leaders wrote a new constitution. It granted civil rights to all citizens. Japanese leaders agreed to never wage war again.

Crimes of War

After the war, several top Japanese leaders were hanged for war crimes. Among their crimes was the abuse of prisoners. Captured soldiers had been forced into hard labor. They were starved and beaten. Around 4 in 10 American prisoners held by Japan died in captivity.

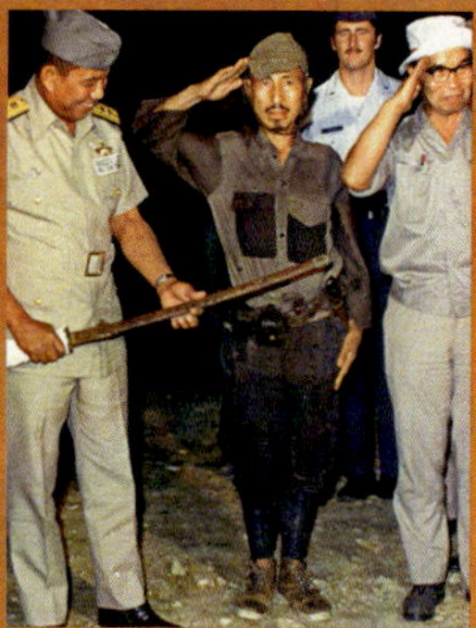

Left Behind

Some Japanese soldiers refused to believe the war was over. They stayed hidden for years. One of those soldiers was Officer Hiroo Onoda (in black above). He hid in the Philippines for almost 30 years. Onoda and others believed that Emperor Hirohito was a god. Therefore, Japan could not have lost. Onoda finally surrendered in 1974.

MacArthur and Hirohito in September 1945

▲ **This sign in Nagasaki today shows how the same view looked in October 1945.**

Japan rebuilt itself with amazing speed. It became a stable democracy. It also developed one of the world's top economies.

Both sides spent years recovering from the war. Many people had died. Whole cities and islands were destroyed. As both sides rebuilt, they grew stronger. Today, the United States has a good relationship with Japan. The former enemies now rely on each other to succeed.

Write It!

In September 1945, General MacArthur was given "supreme command" of the Allied forces. It was his job to shape Japan after the war. For the first two years, MacArthur led an effort to break apart Japan's military. He also shaped a new government. In 1947, the Allies helped to write a new constitution. Some of the major changes included:

1. The emperor would no longer be in charge of the country.
2. Japan could still have an emperor, but only as a symbolic position.
3. All citizens, including women, were given civil rights.
4. Japan could defend itself if attacked but could never initiate a war again.

Imagine you are like MacArthur. You have just fought in the bloodiest war in human history. You are now tasked with helping to rebuild your former enemy. Write your own constitution for the country. Remember to take into account the causes and effects of the war on the country.

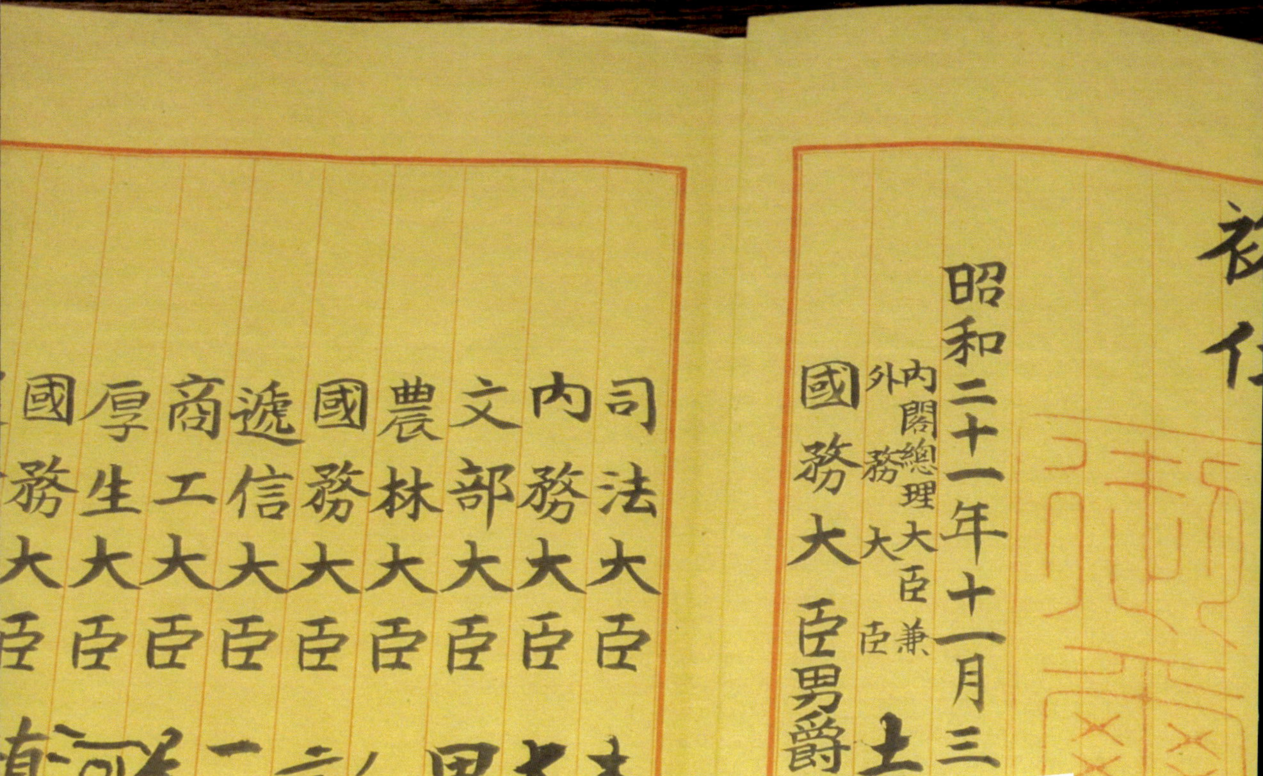

1947 constitution ▲

Glossary

aircraft carriers—warships with flat decks where planes take off and land

airfields—open areas where planes take off and land

ambush—set a trap and wait to attack by surprise

atomic bombs—explosive devices that release energy to create violent explosions

blockade—an act of war in which soldiers or ships are used to stop people and supplies from entering or leaving places

casualties—people who are killed, captured, or seriously injured during warfare

catastrophic—resulting in a massive disaster

embargo—a government order that limits trade

fleet—a group of warships under one management

fronts—areas where active warfare are taking place

infamy—an act known for being evil, shocking, and shameful

intercepted—seized or took something before it could arrive at its planned destination

internment camps—prisons where people are kept for political reasons during wars

kamikaze—refers to an attack whereby the attacker commits suicide by crashing a plane into an enemy target

malaria—a serious disease that is passed by mosquito bites

mushroom cloud—a large cloud of smoke and dust that is caused by the explosion of a nuclear weapon

radiation sickness—a serious illness that is caused by too much exposure to the energy produced by nuclear reactions

stronghold—a place where members of a military can defend against attacks

war crimes—wartime acts that are against international law because they are cruel or unfair

withdrawing—moving away from a threat

Index

Your Turn!

On Friday, February 23, 1945, photographer Joe Rosenthal snapped a photograph in Iwo Jima. Two days later, his photograph was on the cover of Sunday newspapers around the world. The photograph, entitled "Raising the Flag on Iwo Jima," became one of the most famous photos of the war. It went on to win the Pulitzer Prize and was used on stamps and posters.

One fan of Rosenthal's photograph was sculptor Felix W. de Weldon. He created a bronze statue of the image. The statue took years to complete. On November 10, 1954, President Dwight D. Eisenhower unveiled de Weldon's work. It now stands outside the Marine Corps War Memorial in Arlington, Virginia. Each year, around 1.5 million people visit the memorial and see the statue.

Imagine you are in charge of creating a memorial for the Pacific Theater of the war. Sketch a design for a monument or sculpture that you think expresses how people felt during and after the war. Then, build your work of art.